CEAC

TALKING PILLOW

D1593137

PITT POETRY SERIES
ED OCHESTER, EDITOR

TALKING PILLOW

ANGELA BALL

UNIVERSITY OF PITTSBURGH PRESS

Published by the University of Pittsburgh Press, Pittsburgh, Pa., 15260
Copyright © 2017, Angela Ball
All rights reserved
Manufactured in the United States of America
Printed on acid-free paper
10 9 8 7 6 5 4 3 2 1

ISBN 13: 978-0-8229-6515-2
ISBN 10: 0-8229-6515-1

Cover art by Angela Ball
Cover design by Melissa Dias-Mandoly

For Michael

CONTENTS

FBI STORY

BICYCLE STORY

THE LAST TOAST

for Anna Akhmatova

I drink to the narrow window a face peers through at four a.m.,
to the little side road that leads to grief,
to the ones bullied to death,
to the warm logic of the unknown,
to the tall gates, the master's wide,
wide gates, nonexistent and latched forever.

THE LADY OF THE HOUSE

SOCIETY FOR THE LADIES OF THE HOUSE

There was a chapter in Poland before the war.
Now I'm a chapter of me. I study Escoffier,
the delicate art of simmering unclouded broth
courtesy of a *Chinoise*; from Rombauer
the method for rolling dough to the translucency
of a silk stocking. I polish stainless steel
with olive oil, scrub my fingertips with a lemon half
after mincing garlic. The piano waits at attention
for each evening's attempt at Schumann. I unfurl
the newspaper, place it next to the leather chair.
I bring the slippers, fancy ones, rimmed
with Alpine braid. Domesticity rises
through me till I flush like a safe and convenient
battery-powered candle. I read *Ladies' Home
Journal*, "Ten New Ways to Please your Man,"
and memorize each in pantomime. The house approves
of me. It parades the sky in its windows, admits
the opera of passing sirens, the swerving, rocking
ambulance with its brave young driver, determined
to reach the hospital in time to save the patient,
to let him heal and return home, tentative
but upright, to his one true love, the Lady of the House.

LO QUE HAY

I'm just learning about jazz having competing elements
or instruments that speak up for themselves
like strings of pearls, like a girl named Anita.

Also shooting apostrophes with my apostrophe gun
dragging them home to my poetry oasis
playing them my new favorite song
by Arturo Sandoval, *"Eso es lo que hay."*

The question we ask about others: how
is (s)he taking it? For example a widow
part Cherokee married again but he wanted
Charleston she didn't now she has boyfriend very tall
Cubano-Spanish and daughters in twenties, jobs they don't like

but seem happy. The question about ourselves:
how do we get? Uninteresting spiritless
envy; also sense that thing
is not thing, but black-and-white jazz funeral,
we its blowsy handkerchiefs.

BOYFRIEND STORY

The man I had been dating
tossed small stems of narcissus
into a water glass. They looked good.

"That's what you get
for having an artist
as a boyfriend," he said.

Not all I got. Also, anger
For having "ignored" the photos
of his paintings posted on the frig.

I pointed out his lack of response
to pictures I'd emailed of my sister.
He said, "Who cares about that? An older
you, riding a horse."

Cognitive dissonance
happens for a reason. Can make us

break up or down.
Design a glacier bedspread, with protective
scree pillows. Confiscate items
that announce themselves: TEA COZY,
JUDY'S NOTEBOOK, and so on; expunge
monograms, especially the satin appliques
on imperial bathrobes.

Be the sworn protector
of the names written with little stones in the desert,
of KEATS writ in water,

of his cemetery in Rome, so decrepit,
where shadowy cats
loll among the graves, brushing
the faint patronymics
with the gaud of their tails.

SPONTANEOUS AUTOBIOGRAPHICAL REVELATION

"It seems you've had a lot of male
attention," my therapist said.

It hit me: I had craned towards such notice.
It came, trailing

the famous consequences
for those I considered supernumeraries.

Attention escaped in time
through many windows.

Eternities, then
an angel showed up

in the usual fashion:
as an imposition.

As angels go, this one
was undemanding.
No wrestling match,

ladder, far-fetched
pregnancy. No artistic

vision, insisting
I live solo in a castle.

I wouldn't say I was "chosen."
only somehow available,

able to share with a man, a Michael,
the upstart mystery the messenger
placed in my hands.

CAREER

Long ago in Mexico, friends said that I could make a living as a singer. All I needed was to dye my hair blonde, get a guitar, and memorize some songs. My American accent would make me irresistibly childish. I declined to be adorable, but now I change my mind. Welcome, days of reading and writing notes for poems—or songs—in cafés set in arcades along the principal streets. Welcome, nights of singing "Jealous of the Moon" badly but charmingly into the eyes and faces of strangers. Welcome, waiters called "*Tigre*" bringing *pulque con piña,* sweet and nourishing. My height would be alarming, but would add to the contrasts of my act. By my calculation the show could persist for twenty years, at which time I would take a room in a tall building and wait for the guitar's thickest string to vibrate with the earth.

UNFORMED PERSONALITY DISORDER (UPD)

You never twigged that social skills must be taught
sooner than tap or kickball.

The teacher who said "If you don't ask a boy to dance,
you're going to the principal's office" didn't twig, either.

Satan needed a sanctum and chose the gym locker room,
with girl devils that specialized in ridicule of the specific.

Your career has varied. On Silk Street
you were nearly flattened. By distraction and lorry.

For a time, you bored or discomfited many people, serially.
For a time, you admired the Amish. And their apparent rules.

The trick, if there is one, isn't to "see yourself as others
See you." It is to see others.

You learned from Frank O'Hara in an astonished poem
that he, too, was a child pariah.

Two deer come to the lawn. Their legal address is the woods.
One of them is probably Frank.

TALKING PILLOW

A pillow talked to me.
It stood on end and spoke.
It did not have a mouth.
A pillow has no mouth.

The pillow said, "We do not like the kapok
we like the goose down. We like
the deft fingers of women
to handle our fabrication."

Said, "Your last love was best.
He is gone. We bear
no responsibility
nor will we bear any
in future."

Said, "This is a matter of fate."

Fate said, "This is your silence.
It will conform to you."

WHAT IS PLEASURE

The supreme pleasure of love
is the knowledge of *doing evil*.
We know that all voluptuousness
makes its home there.

There are other pleasures.

That of watching
twelve or fourteen leagues of liquid
in constant movement.

That of contemplating nomadic peoples,
who in their native dignity
know nothing of mediocrity, or the desire
to converse with Satan in the form
of a dog or cat, or the belief in progress
which means that others
will do our work and thank us
for the pleasure.

That of knowing superstition
is the well of truth; and, how in Paris,
in every grand theatre
the chandelier is the protagonist—

really a spellbound whore
who enjoys flying up at the right moment,
opening herself utterly,
taking all requests.

BASSFIELD BLUE

Paint has a history
        sometimes deep blue—

saying itself up and down a street,
        stoop, doorframe, window sash,

like a thought running one to the next.
        A house-to-house handyman

offering small jobs.
        The partial suited me—a wife here,

a child there, various tries. Sounds came
        hand to mouth:

A grackles' evening of furious
        playground swings, a seethe of salt

in the bottom of a bag,
        blue.

YOU SAY IT'S HARD TO JOIN THE HOURS

You say it's hard to join the hours,
you've lost the plot. Some hints:

Do not put baklava into a briefcase.

Don't apologize for potatoes, the way one woman
did: "All the big ones go to restaurants."

Don't dry a bridge
with a dishcloth.

Don't sweep the street
every which way, like a responsible madwoman.

Don't scream insults at passing mirrors.

Think how privileged you are
to seldom stand waiting
for a car to come.

That your house belongs to Google Earth.

Think what it was to blow into a first instrument,
follow a melody.

Listen to pines as they make the sound called "soughing."
Listen to birds fluting dawn into law.

THE LITTLE TOWNS HOIST ON ONE SHOULDER

Surveyors arrived first
with their chains and tripods:

"The towns will be well served
by their rivers." Floods swept in

engineers, who laced the channels
straight, restrung the bridges.

The little towns
have squandered their sidewalks,

torn apart their dime stores:
brassieres strong-armed to parts unknown,

batons twirled beyond our atmosphere
to the planet of majorettes.

The little towns captain limestone oceans.
They voyage in place, guided through dark waves
by the sails of their names.

SOME REGRETS THAT WILL ATTEND YOU WHEN YOU MAY HAVE KICKED THE SEAT OF THE PATRON IN FRONT OF YOU AT THE MOVIE THEATER TOO OFTEN

A sad milkman drops the milk
and enters a strange basement
to use the restroom. A repentant fox runs past,
looking transparent like a slide of fire.

"A hell of an out," they say
in these parts, referring to the green caterpillar
with brown spikes found exploring the Chef's Salad
on two separate occasions, despite
the guardianship of saltines, and referring, too,
to the Galaxy that fell off its wheels
inconveniently.

At the movies
you are disappointed at your failure
to stop kicking the seat
of the person in front of you,
and take your leg outside, where it continues
its protest. The bath mat in your backpack
is a lamentable gift
for your true love, a contrite ghost who has gotten
lost in the dark, a guilty river that
follows the concrete, a dejected sneeze
gone free.

The man who breaks dirty dishes
and buys new ones is as mournful
as were bewailed the happy campers
who threw their smug song up our penitent noses.
But when Brenda Lee's record falls,
when Brenda Lee's record falls,
she is Commissar of Sorry.

SPORADIC GUN CATALOGUE WITH LINE FROM "GERONTION"

This weapon
causes kinetic damage
penalty to impact
After such knowledge
fire drift control
this weapon has bonus
accuracy when firing

from the hip
upgrade damage extra
precision damage
such knowledge
this weapon has control
enhanced impact single point

sling rounds stagger
recoil low cannon fire this weapon has
damage attack
balance kinetic penalty
perfect smart drift
what forgiveness?

Discerning shooters choose a weapon
to suit their unfolding knowledge,
and the sports that have engaged them as fans.
Skeet, hunting: duck, squirrel, or bounty
require distinct calibers, margins of forgiveness
for hand-eye miscommunication, damage

to the barrel, a sudden limb fall that damages
the line of sight, a bodily vibration reaching the weapon,
perhaps a flurry of additional prey, a forgiveness
in order of flight obscures the original target, the knowledge
attaching it to clear sky, a single bounty
present for the taking as its wings catch air and fan.

ELEGY

"She has a knee,"
the TSA agent said.
A pat-down situation—legs
in wrong position. One forward,
no, back. No arms
overhead. Same strokes
for all.

First flight since the insertion
of a prosthetic knee, first since vacation
in a cabin named "Golden Memories."

I was watching the movie Michael chose for me,
Scandal Sheet, 1952, with Broderick Crawford and Donna Reed.
Michael was in the bathroom, place of danger. Was,
in fact, dying.

The squad arrived, positioned him,
applied the riveting voltage.

A tech set my I-pad
to the address but I didn't know
how to start route. Place with name
of hospital was shopping mall, closed.
Where Saint Dolly is a billboard,
a serene welcome, a beige lace bodice with a feint
of cleavage. How nice for her
to be outside all the time,
part of the scenery.

An hour or so before the attack
Michael had suggested we go the next day
to a magic show. At this, heart sank. Mouth said, "Sure,
I'll go with you."

What magic now and never, what baton,
mirror, slipped lock?

Arrived at Emergency, the first of grief's little rooms
with its fresh supply of tissues. I didn't see Michael.
He was being prepped
for transport to the city:
a pallet swung, a spinneret of wings.

I drove after, to the big hospital. Shut all down
one side, as if by stroke.

His chute-like bed. The black
board's goal of the day:
Wean From Ventilator.

When visiting hours ended, I was shown
to a room filled with grief's La-Z-Boys,
grief's Barcaloungers. People on and off
cellphones.

The day before, we had cruised the drag
of Gatlinburg. It occurred to me that now
we would surely never attend
the "All-You-Can-Eat Lumberjack Feud
Dinner Theater," or dine again at the over-hyped
restaurant, its patio with a creek
like a bandaged pet stretched alongside.

State of the patient's brain unknown,
on the second day its controls sputtered,
dials spinning, thermostats deceived—
the board erased. "Your partner is very ill,"
the nurse said.

The summons. The neurologists' announcement:

"We feel we can be direct with you."

—"Just enough brain stem for some respiration.
        Imagine an aperture retracting, receding
        as at the end of a cartoon."

"Always assume that they can hear"

The brain, swirling with movies, had starved
into itself. All medicine too late,
though the heart pulsed, stented.
Unstinting.

Breath held too long while my eyes and brain took in
Scandal Sheet, while Michael was scandalously
alone then more
much more alone.

*

Death deranges the shoe size. The formal wingtips
would not fit. No matter. So apropos, the dark suit,
the Jesuit School tie
with mascot Blue Jays
midflight.

I was left alone with him, tissues
within reach.

To the touch, marble-like.
Not the igneous stone—
the spherical toy
knuckled down into dirt.

He had talked of his drawstring bag
of keepsies, ushered by manmade flood
down the 17th-street canal. Tigers,
Swirlies, Deep Blue Seas,
Green Ghosts.

He had talked of the New Orleans that called out:
Knife Sharpener, Genuine Hot Waffles, Taffy Wagon,
Haha the Icecream Man, Haha of today's flavors.

Our trip to the mountains doesn't end,
though Michael was flown to MSY in an outsized shoebox,
Human Remains. No seat selection,
no view, no warmth to lean against.

Doesn't end, though I wrote
the owners of "Golden Memories"
that my partner had died,
and the Jacuzzi, with its surcharge,
remained unused.

Let me hear that Michael hears.
In his fashionable Tiny House,

His burial plot in Metairie Cemetery,
near what was once the finish line
of the city racetrack,
he hears the chorus of wagers,
percussion of hoof beats
over hoof beats, the quiet
of laid dust.

I travel, searching the perfect vacancy.
I have sent memories out ahead. They gleam.
I have sent a knee.

FBI STORY

STATUS

A black enameled Singer
guarded the spinster's room.

Its painted garlands hinted
the distant beauty of pianos.

Through threads of rain,
a hearse passed, bearing its slanted S.

The spinsters lived in a row. We were not
pretty. Our work was close,
the day, a thread
knotted at one end.

SORCERERS

A country of watery drugs
and amateur magic,
flowers bred to speak Latin.

The garden could tell
what was in our minds:
a large roast, a silken tassel,
a bruised walking stick.

We encountered dead mist and a new,
bitchy concierge, also a fortuneteller,

who said. "Your fame will follow the war
that heals you; you will stain a flag; your children
will destroy a footbridge by means
of harmonic motion."

We knew who we were when
we jumped up and down on one question.

Our favorite magician turned himself into a wheezy cocktail siphon,
then into a cedar, the tallest of trees, then into a white horse
falling from a bridge.

THE WOMAN WHO WORKS IN THE MEDICAL SUPPLY STORE IS STRANGE. SO IS A DETECTIVE.

An envelope only for keys
came with the job.
The store is pre-fab,
unvaried. Not operatic.
Shelves have flags and arrows
pointing to needs. Unguents,
capes, medicinal forevers.
Autopsies planted at birth.

A phone call about a customer's prosthesis:
"Could she be hiding
her real arm behind her back
like Lon Chaney?"
The caller is a detective.
Deals in flagrant
disclosures, theaters of morals.
His storefront has a window
with two dolls in bed. A third doll,
with magnifying glass,
pokes out from under. A happy
family.

The Medical Supply Store magnifies
night. But gauze denies it.
A single crutch leans into a corner
like a fallen branch into the crotch
of its father.

ON DISENCUMBERMENTATIONALISM

Copy the husband who disappeared
to conceal himself next to the house,
become a pair of eyes
as a wolfish woman moved
ever more slowly
through lamp-lit rooms.
Let her find you, but only
after you have become a cat.
Or, if you are modern,
try seventeen occupations,
each of which requires a new alphabet
and going to school with thousands
of retooled geniuses. Place bets on cardboard horses
that lurch forward toward heartbreaking loss.
Tell Fortune you're fine, watch her float out to sea
tied bravely to her little stick.

FBI STORY

One day my car got a flat. I was foolish.
I entered the car of a strange man
who said he would take me to a shop he knew,
and someone would return with us
to fix the tire. We rode past many rags
of snow; the man spoke of his career
in fashion. I asked, "Would you please
take me home?" He did. The next day,
when I received the anonymous letter
demanding I appear barefoot at the reservoir,
I did not venture to guess
who it was from. Instead, I called the police.

They sat on my couch, passed the letter around.
"You have not yet been harmed. There is nothing
we can do. But tomorrow, call the Postal Inspector."
I did, and was connected immediately
with the FBI. The Federal Bureau
of Investigation. The FBI repairman
came and fixed my tire, talking of
weather. Then I was instructed to enter a specific
phone booth, call a number. A voice asked,

"Are you willing to go to the reservoir? We will wait
in the bushes."
—"Only if I have to."
"That's OK," the voice said. We have an agent
whose build resembles yours. Do you wear hats?
She will wear a hat and sunglasses."

She wore them when I handed her
my identity. This happened behind a movie house,
the men driving black Plymouths,
the woman taking the keys
to my white Pontiac 350 V-8 with its discreet
racing stripe.

I left town, got a call: the plan had worked. The agent
got into the man's car, flashed her badge, and there was
a high-speed chase. "Randall says he knows you," the agent said.
Yes. You guessed correctly. It was the man who had given me
the useless ride. Randall, an air force recruit
preoccupied with bathing. His note had demanded

I appear in fresh clothing with clean buttons
up the front. It said that if I did not show,
he would get me or his many friends would get me.

Randall pled guilty to Extortion. I do not know
what happened then. He could be anywhere.
The chief agent visited me, said, "I am glad
that you are not my daughter. Here is my card.
If you ever need help, call this number."

The card was fire and joke proof. I kept it
under the hat I did not wear
until it had served its time.

ANCESTRAL DENTURES

A dentist filled a woman's mouth
with teeth of a hanged man.
Again, her jaws furious
with bread.

As the man was hauled to the gallows
in an open wagon
stopping at every pub, crowds
of unrecognized devils had shouted,

"Free drink for the condemned!"
The man held onto a glass, thought
of the future his full set of teeth
would endure. How they might miss
his favorite sweetmeat,
nougatine. His bright tongue.

Teeth whose only crime had been to bite
a nursemaid, and that forgiven at once,
in the same instant.

BILLET DOUX

A woman writes, "We can meet at the car dealer's
if you want." They pretend to be married, shopping for
        transport.

On a particular retaining wall
at the bend of an exit, blurry boys spray paint
love over love.

A walk along the sea must skirt the lines
of jealous fishermen
guarding their silver.

A woman says, "A transistor radio
was my first love." Her body directed
through a primitive earpiece.

The great cities hunt their sisters
with mixed success.
It's hard for them to throw a voice,

pressed as they are
on their seaboards,
like too many adult teeth.

TO LON CHANEY IN *THE UNKNOWN*

The circus knows that animals are not infants,
but laws.

Lon, armless knife thrower, your Spanish hat
judges the hard silence.

Your natural arms not gone, but bound.
When Nanon, the inchoate
Joan Crawford, said that she felt imperially safe
in your non-arms, your fanaticism
believed, bribed a surgeon, returned you

in triumph to horror, her: subsumed
in the Strong Man's vast,
hairy appendages. Your brain a storm
of hoops, condemned tents,
hushed deaths of the quadripedal. Dear

Lon,
Nanon did not love you for your missing
arms, your arms loved you missing.

The Unknown needs no arms. Only the blade
inside the blade, the sternness.

HER EYES

With her eyes' iridescence
I blindfolded my vanished cur
and tucked a cartoon bone
under my chin.

With whitest pines
I blindfolded a hill
bitten and slipping.
I hide as I go, show myself
in various enamels, in bird milk,
in the motion of climbing, the motion
of lying down.

COUNTRY OF SONGBIRDS

After Elinor's death, Robert Frost wrote,
"Birdsong will never be the same."
True for Robert.
                    For others, not
so much. We depart and workarounds kick
in. Sombreros on birthdays, bonus
                            Mariachis, the same.
        Same
leaves and hair molting; zeniths
and nadirs; the blood and the harvest; the Circadian;
Mercator's projection and Newton's tidy machine
creaky but functional; how things move
                            or refuse; dawn's water buffalo
led forward, yoked with milk,
hooves' raw sucking
till the mud lets go.

REMARKS YOU MAY HAVE PREPARED FOR THE DINNER

Look at her. She isn't hungry.

You know how it is when
someone you are with isn't hungry—

picks at her food, or maybe some coal
or nearby pavement—

Excuse me, does this by any chance contain
potash or sundries? I'm allergic

to sundries, especially anything
the color of baby chicks. Is this a premises?

If so, we may have to leave. I think
I'm feeling queasy.

Could you just wrap up one of those lamps
for me? And that table over there?

The one with all the legs and teeth marks?
I love those so.

METHODS OF CHOICE

In Miss Elbow's class, late Friday afternoon, we played
Orchestra. The piano gave us "Charming Village,"
a version that ate its own tail. A box opened with a flourish,
we chose our instruments.

                                            The tambourine the pet.
The triangle the queen. The woodblock the drudge,
with its rude stick. We didn't think it made music.

                                                    When struck,
its low thwock went straight to the xylem and phloem
of trunks, to a harsh clearing,
branches tumbling a slough.

                                    Dumb block, singing itself
to the incapable, the ones who would grow up
prizing the showy, the uncaring.

YOUNG BENEFACTOR

The benefactor's identity is not secret,
though I like to pretend so.
He smiles personably, far away. I think he would enjoy
the scene of these pines beside the highway
as they saturate slowly with darkness
that makes the sky paler and pinker,
and the piled machinery of that quarry,
a high mouth for dirt and small stones
pouring a perfect triangle
that should not be disturbed.

The day in junior high when I tried small talk
with a popular girl: "I haven't seen you lately."
"—I should give you a photograph," or during the Ninth-
grade Trip, when I sat alone, the Odd
Number, someone should have told me:
Your benefactor is being born.

AN ATTEMPT

For us, all that's left
is a dried bee, tilted
onto one wing.

Not long ago, a bloom
fastened its tongue, while its belly
tried unsuccessfully
to tip it backwards.

We mustn't touch—
anything without water
is without give.

This bee is our scout—
one day, dust
will pronounce itself
in the armatures
of every flower.
But we'll not be closer.

BICYCLE STORY

PHENOMENAL BODY

The far reaches need gathering in.
"Springtime, and the first birds and letters reach
the lonely Arctic."

The left hand with its jimmied fingers.
The right hand crooking a cup's ear.

The changes. The feet more serious,
the toes more chary.

Bridge I love you says the pelvis.
Knee asks how ships balance
on the world's great canals.

The body packed with travel. Gallop of the circulatory,
lanes and flyways of the lymphatic, the glandular, the nervous.

The back of the head nonplussed
never to know itself directly,
within it the pituitary of the nine secretions,
the multiple dynamic equilibriums.

The eyes' individual oceans
shadowed with debris. The retinas,
forward parts of the brain.

The forehead's masonic third eye, messenger
of morning twilight.

LOTS OF SWEARING AT THE FAIRGROUNDS

The stable hands and cart drivers.

The trotters, rosettes on their bridles.

Their carts, small bites
from a buckboard.

The track a wreath of dust
tacked to the earth.

At the fairgrounds even children
were full of curses, scrawled across mornings.

What was denied: open pasture,
the perfection of a stallion covering a mare.

BRING THE GREATEST FOOD TO THE GREATEST HUMANS

You must devise a system of menus, catalogues,
and rates of exchange for all denominations
of taste and their fond opposites,
and toss copies out of airplanes.
Remember, *Pneumatics*
Can be traced back to Hero of Alexandria.

In Michel and Jules Verne's *The Day of an American Journalist,*
in 2889 submarines will carry people faster than aerotrains,
while the Society for Supplying Food to the Home
assembles and delivers pneumatic meals.

Water tables may present difficulties,
but, with your help, soon, we will arrive
at work in perfect moods, with lunch
swooshing its way underground
from the most radiant lands.

Love, gastronomy, velocity.
the ABCs. Meringues whiz past
our forebears.

A LAST STAY

Hospital—"God's hostel"—construct
of corners, my assigned bed seven stories

(the cancer floor) above ground
I won't walk on again. Hall a sleeve

of prophylactic coolness, room connected by buzzer
to the nurses' station, where personnel fall back

for orders, supplies. My live name
begins to revisit itself
letter by letter. A noon

beyond reach of morphine.
God of Sleep
becoming permanent.

The dreamlike undying world:
a forest where lions scratch.

A public pool, a child
swimming for the first time
underwater.

THE RIVER WANTS GRIP

But each river loosens.

A prison wants people to behave.
Wants to slowly crush
with its smooth anvil.

A city wants a long moment
as a horse drawing reins
of water
between its teeth.

An asylum is a museum
of people. It wants to be
an avalanche.

A hospital is a ship
that must huff its sails
and snap flags.

These passengers let off
at bilious docks
get music to flaunt
above their trouble.

SPRINGTIME

When bees start bumping into each other, she remembers that man, the salesman thought so "promising," such a "good person," who took her for a ride in his convertible. She failed to react promptly to his sudden "advances"—as she had similarly failed to react to the transparent eyes of the lumberman, the tongue of the optometrist, the hands from behind in the movie house.

LISTEN: *Apart from helium, and probably neon, all gases that can be breathed*

The men who detained her without explanation

LISTEN: *have a narcotic effect, which is greater as the lipid solubility of the gas*

May themselves have been captives, automatons, beings warped into behaving JUST ONE WAY.

LISTEN: *increases. As depth increases, the effects may become hazardous as*

The prisoner wanted to be the agile woman she heard of who jumped from a window and fled across the roofs of Madrid, leaving the WOULD-BE rapist lost.

LISTEN: *the diver is increasingly impaired. Although divers can learn to cope with the effects, it is not possible to develop a tolerance. While narcosis affects all divers, predicting the depth at which narcosis will affect a diver is difficult, as susceptibility varies widely from dive to dive and amongst individuals. Narcosis can produce tunnel vision, making it difficult to read multiple gauges.*

She was twenty.

LEISURE

If you go for a drive, know
      that small roadside crosses
contain your friends, re-mastered.
      Respect reports of pain
from every other planet.
      Let your cigarette sparkle
in energetic blackness.

INTERCOURSE AFTER DEATH PRESENTS SPECIAL DIFFICULTIES

I love you, I want to have sex
with you. It is so damned awkward.
So many explanations
required, having to stare down
the salacious and insist
on a conjugal visit to the after-

life. Nothing like a movie: some sexy actress
roped in pearls, masturbating to a dime-store
photograph. Nothing like ancient Egypt, men with false
penises attached to their mummies, action ready.

Just us, equipped with pairs of shadow towels and toothbrushes,
an immense bedchamber kitted out
for the impossible, the invisible,
the never-again, the at-no-time.

Nights I ingest the pill
that lets me seem awake while in motion
at home and at work. I note
today's horoscope:
"a far-fetched hope is realized."

WHAT HAPPENS TO WOMEN

Hours of women
tie up herds of tamales and polish
the skyscrapers of the potent.

Their radiant forceful bodies
float beatifically through the poetry
of Khalil Gibran,

wander half-crazed mountains,
find flowers hiding other flowers,
bears stuck to each other with sleep.

At six p.m., an indigo of women
flows south across London Bridge.
Cufflinks sweep past
in knowledgeable black cabs.

Orpheus's lyre, plucking by itself,
plays across seas, destroyers following it,
fish following it, a snafu of tornados,
hailstorms, northern lights.
Eurydice listens, listens not.

THE WOMAN ON MEXICO STREET

My house is here,
roof like the Virgin's cloak,
interior bright with the ghost
of bleach: a high, noiseless whine.

We're having hurricane spring: various skeletons
modeling honeysuckle. Dogwoods full length
on the ground, blooming their funeral.

The street owns more dogs
than people. The dogs and I don't recognize
each another. They run, dragging
invisible chains. I sit tight

With supplies of food
and thoughts that come back
like dogs. The bowl of dog food
empties by morning. The bowl of thoughts,
never. Like the shore,

I've taken early retirement.
We're all headed to the sea,
so why wait? Because, God knows,
the water is cold
and can't be trusted.

LANDSCAPE AFTER GOING

Lake Forgetful streaked umber,
clouds upside down in scuds, inmates
of water. Armadillos, one and another,
getting along.

No drooping sunflower, no red stake
driven into an edge, no shadow
of muddy spring, no house
an accidental statue.

But the memory that all along
I had stood my plain case
on a man's foot in the crowd and he had said
nothing, that in a high window a dog's face
had been watching.

TESTIMONY

I saw my love pull up at the bank .
of summer, exchange steaming corn
for cherries, while cool
teased warm in spring's Laundromat
splendid with crushed blooms.
I saw him enter the continent
of a pond. I saw her hit a triple
for the Apricot Stars.
I saw him enter a scented booth.
I saw her at the shrimp dance. "We must be intense
to make intensity," the shrimp said. I saw him
at the hops picking, I tore down vines,
stripped their nubs in the big fields, adding bitter
to sweet, until time to walk back
into the deep of the city and its dimmer
ways. The custom of holding a button
in deference to a passing hearse. No button,
no luck. Tossing cats, dodging salt,
none of it matters. The custom of passing the baton,
watching it tumble high, all elbows,
into the depths of luck, silver-ribbed,
a single jack.

SECOND ELEGY

The first death was attended by a joke photo
of the actor, Don Knots, as Barney Fife.
Gun drawn.

The second by daughter, sister-in-law,
partner, and sidelined ventilator.

It is fitting that widows, like the *Veuve Clicquot,*
make bubbly. They know the value
of good air.

During the Vietnam War, Michael sued the State
for the return of his body, won. No suit
this time.

No State can return his eyes, hazel
of unknown provenance,
macedonia of green, brown, gold,
the gift of Rayleigh scattering—that which blues
the sky.

He has fallen through stage boards into the trap room.
Been dragged by devils through a door in a rock.
Died in battle because wearing loose armor.

Heart made as if to leave
without him; then, he left,
taking heart away
from work.

It is rumored that you cross
two rivers. A ferryman conducts
the boat. In this case,
a good idea.

The male drivers of Michael's family
shared one trait: unconditional animus
for fellow motorists. Sin of sins:
Following Too Closely. The freeway response:
Slow Down. The street response:
Pull Over Brusquely,
let the bastard pass.

BICYCLE STORY

I rode a bicycle. I rode it well
and fast. One day it crashed,
I don't know why. All was dark
then I got up and started riding again.
Knew that I would be having
lunch soon with two friends. Did not know
who I was. Even so, the trail was pretty,
with mysterious berries and weeds perched
every which way. A turkey vulture,
afloat in the gap between treetops, righted itself.
A wing swept low, a torn page.
On it I read my name.

NOTES

"What Is Pleasure": Charles Baudelaire wrote in his *Intimate Journals* that "the unique and supreme pleasure of making love lies in the certitude of doing evil."

"Springtime": The italicized lines are derived from a Wikipedia entry for nitrogen narcosis, also called "raptures of the deep" and the "Martini effect."

ACKNOWLEDGMENTS

Grateful acknowledgment is made to the editors of the following journals, in which several of the poems in this manuscript originally appeared:

August 1: "Some Regrets That May Attend You When You Have Kicked the Seat of the Patron in Front of You at the Movie Theater Too Often"; *The Best American Poetry* blog: "Intercourse after Death Presents Special Difficulties," "Second Elegy"; *Blip*: "What Happens to Women"; *Boulevard*: "Talking Pillow"; *Cincinnati Review*: "Remarks You May Have Prepared for the Dinner," "Testimony," "Phenomenal Body," "You Say It's Hard to Join the Hours"; *Colorado Review*: "Lo Que Hay"; *Congeries*: "Sorcerers"; *Field*: "The Little Towns Hoist on One Shoulder," "The River Wants Grip," "A Last Stay," "Billet Doux," "Methods of Choice," "Lots of Swearing at the Fairgrounds," "Unformed Personality Disorder (UPD)," "The Woman Who Works in a Medical Supply Store Is Strange. So Is a Detective"; *Hearths*: "On Disencumbermentationalism"; *Hurricane Blues* (edited by Philip Kolin and Susan Swartout, Southeast Missouri State University, 2006): "The Woman on Mexico Street"; *Laurel Review*: "Rest-Stop Suicide"; *The New Yorker*: "The Last Toast"; *Ploughshares*: "An Attempt"; *Plume*: "What Is Pleasure," "Ancestral Dentures"; *Poetry South*: "What Happens to Women," "Sorcerers," "Some Regrets That Will Attend You When You May Have Kicked the Seat of the Patron in Front of You Too Often," "Bassfield Blue"; *Story* magazine: "For Lon Chaney in *The Unknown*"; *Valley Voices*: "Young Benefactor," "Sporadic Gun Catalogue with Line from 'Gerontion.'"

My thanks to the many friends and colleagues who provided support and inspiration during the writing of this book, including (but not limited to) Frederick Barthelme, Melanie Barthelme, Steven Barthelme, Susan Elliott Brown, Allison Campbell, Timothy Donnelly, Hannah Dow, Rie Fortenberry, Rebecca Morgan Frank, Monika Gehlawat, Brandi George, Jessica Guzman, Theresa Hallgarten, Tony Hallgarten, Luis Iglesias, Julia Johnson, David Lehman, Stacey Harwood Lehman, Todd Osborne, Andrea Spofford, Anastasia Stelse, and Dara Wier.

Thanks always to the family of Michael Leonard Helwick (1946–2015), especially his mother, the late Gertrude Helwick; his daughter, Stephanie Helwick; his sister-in-law, Caroline Helwick; and his nieces, Erica Helwick Doyle and Diana Helwick Stokes.